VINTAGE SEWING ATTACHMENTS FOR THE MODERN SEWIST

BARBARA EMODI

www.ingramcontent.com/pod-product-compliance
Lightning Source LLC
Chambersburg PA
CBHW021809150726

47989CB00004B/1840

CONTENTS

INTRODUCTION TO THE VINTAGE SEWING ROOM

The modern sewist does not work in isolation.

With her in spirit are those who sewed before her - home sewers who made clothing for themselves, their families, friends, neighbors, and dressmaking clients. The skills of these women are part of our heritage as modern makers. I believe the richness of our own current sewing experience can benefit from a connection to that culture. One way we can do that is by rediscovering the most essential tools in the vintage sewing room - classic sewing machine attachments.

This book is an introduction to the machine attachments that were most widely used on domestic sewing machines between 1920 and 1965. These beautifully built, designed, and ingenious tools are still very useful today.

I often use vintage attachments in my own sewing.

I find they make many challenging jobs easier and faster. The very high quality of the work they produce has also made me reconsider the broader idea of progress.

Is newer always better?

The lovely buttonholes and exquisite hems that my older attachments produce have made me wonder. What other older, but superior technologies have we let drift away with our quick replacement culture? Sewing gives a person time to ponder these issues. The prolific home seamstresses of the past sewed more and better, than most of us do now, with machines that were far more basic, simply because they used these attachments.

Sometimes, when I struggle with a detailed sewing challenge, I am awed that some clever mind, operating in another time and place, has already solved my problem for me. Smart thinking and good ideas reach out across many spaces. To use these attachments is to catch some of that and to feel a profound respect for the inventors. Fortunately, these tools are still available, either as vintage originals or, in some cases, in reproduction form, today.

HOW TO FIND AND USE VINTAGE ATTACHMENTS

These tools can be found on eBay and Etsy, at thrift stores, and in boxes of attachments sold with older machines at yard sales. However, most people no longer know how to use them and, as a result, many have been abandoned in decluttering operations.

That is good news for the rest of us. I have never paid more than a few dollars for any of my classic attachments.

TWO OPTIONS FOR ATTACHING VINTAGE FEET TO A MACHINE

Option one: An older machine dedicated to sewing with these tools

This is my preferred approach – it all just fits together better. Basic second-hand machines are easy to find and inexpensive. Older Kenmores, Singer Featherweights, Singer Rocketeers, and 800 series Berninas are my favorites.

Older machines were made of metal. A good cleaning, oiling, and a new needle may be all they need to get them up and running. One of my own favorite machines, a 1960 Singer Rocketeer made in Quebec, was stored in an unheated garage for decades of Canadian winters. Even still, it only took the labors of a six-year-old and me, plus a box of cotton swabs, to clean and oil it to perfection. That machine, like many other older models, has a superb straight stitch.

The secret of the superior quality of the vintage machine straight stitch is that these machines were not designed for our current wide zigzags. As a result, the smaller opening in the vintage throat plate holds the fabric very securely (no wobbling over a big empty hole) to create a more secure and reliable straight stitch.

Option two: Adapt your modern machine to take vintage feet

Vintage feet can also be attached to a contemporary sewing machine if a shank adaptor is used. This adaption is necessary because most new machines have a high shank (the length of the needle bar onto which the foot attaches) and snap-on feet. Vintage machines, on the other hand, almost all have low shanks and use screw-on feet. The exceptions to this rule are the slant needle shank and feet, most notably Singer's Slant-o-matic series of the sixties, and Bernina's distinctive and unique sleeve attachment system for feet (available in "old style" feet used on vintage machines and "new style" for machines produced after 1998.) Note it is often possible to buy adapters that will convert many styles of feet so they can be used on a Bernina, but not possible to convert a Bernina foot to a non-Bernina machine.

In any case, to fit most older attachments to a contemporary machine you may need to find an appropriate shank adapter or extender to attach the screw-on low shank or slant feet to your modern machine. To find the right shank adapter for your model look for sewing machine dealers who work on older machines and or search online sellers like www.sewing-machinesplus.com

A shank adapter looks like this:

However very old machines, like treadles or rotary hooks like the classic Whites, use feet that attach with a toe clamp. These feet will fit only those machines and cannot be adapted to any others. Toe clamp feet look like this:

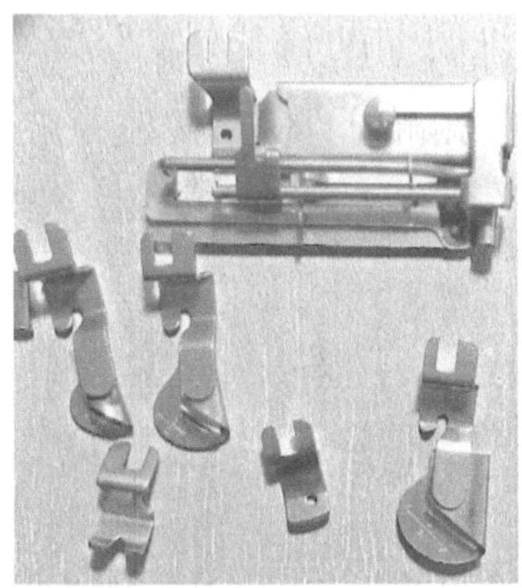

CARE AND MAINTENANCE OF VINTAGE FEET

Compared to their modern counterparts, vintage attachments are impressively well-engineered. Often all it takes is a dusting before they can be used. Only those attachments with moving parts, like the ruffler and the buttonholer, need oiling. Simply add a drop of oil at any point where you see metal moving against metal.

Chapter One

THE VINTAGE ACCESSORY TOOLBOX

I have written this book is not a definitive guide to all older sewing machine attachments, but a practical operator's manual for those most useful in the construction of the clothes we wear today. My emphasis is on high-quality vintage attachments. That said, it should also be acknowledged that many of the tools described here are still manufactured and sold for contemporary machines, notably narrow hemmers, binders, and rufflers. Of these, only the ruffler, and some of the narrow hem feet, are similar quality to their vintage counterparts. (Modern binders are quite less sophisticated than earlier iterations).

Apart from modern versions of the binder, ruffler, and narrow hemmer, all the other attachments discussed here exist only in their vintage form – all excellent examples of "lost technology."

In experimenting with vintage sewing machine attachments it is helpful to understand one core concept – the more complex, even strange, a tool might look, the more ingenious, effective, and simple to use it is.

In learning to use these tools it is helpful to understand

how they work. They can be categorized by three foundational operating principles:

1. Feet that lift or manipulate fabric to reduce its length. These include gathering, shirring, tucker, and pleating feet in their many variations. These feet work by exaggerating the natural action of the feed dogs, either by pressing the fabric into them to force pick up, as in the case of the shirring foot, or by using stitch length to form tiny pleats that look like gathers or mini pleats, as in the ruffler.

2. Feet that fold under raw edges. These feet can look intimidating but are easy to use. Think of the scrolls or brackets on these attachments as tiny extra hands that hold or set up the fabric so it can be stitched with greater control, accuracy, and regularity. The edge stitcher, narrow hemmer, and adjustable hemmer fall into this category.

3. Attachments that are template-driven. Because of the bulk of templates, these tools move the fabric underneath them in many directions to place stitches with precision under the needle. This enables the highly accurate stitching of the legendary vintage buttonhole as well as complex decorative embroideries like monograms and motifs. The quality of the template buttonhole in my view has yet to be surpassed in quality by even the most expensive modern computerized machines.

I have listed each of the most useful attachments in each category in alphabetical order.

Chapter Two

THE ADJUSTABLE HEMMER

CONCEPT

Although the adjustable hemmer looks very complex, it is a very straightforward tool.

It is made of two parts - at the front, a hem depth measuring scale and, at the back, a hem folder-underer. (I hope you can follow the technical terminology).

Once set up, the adjustable hemmer will turn under the raw edge of the hem allowance and situate it under the needle to stitch an exquisitely tiny and precise distance from that edge. And it does this while, at the same time, it holds and folds down the larger hem allowance. Incredibly this all happens without any pre-pressing or pinning necessary.

HOW IT WORKS

The adjustable hemmer can be used with the measuring ruler engaged to fold under and stitch hems from 1/8" to 1". To use, hand press under the raw edge at the top of the hem allowance and then insert the whole hem so it is under the scale, butted up right to the marked number as far as you can feel it go. Once this is done, just lower the presser foot and stitch.

Finished hem, wrong side, see how close the stitches are to the folded under raw edge.

With the measuring ruler moved to the left and front, possible when the screw that attaches it is loosened, the adjustable hemmer can also be used to stitch down much wider hems, although the hem allowance will need to be turned under and pressed in this case as the hemmer will be active only to turn under and stitch the raw edge of the hem allowance. This is how that looks in operation:

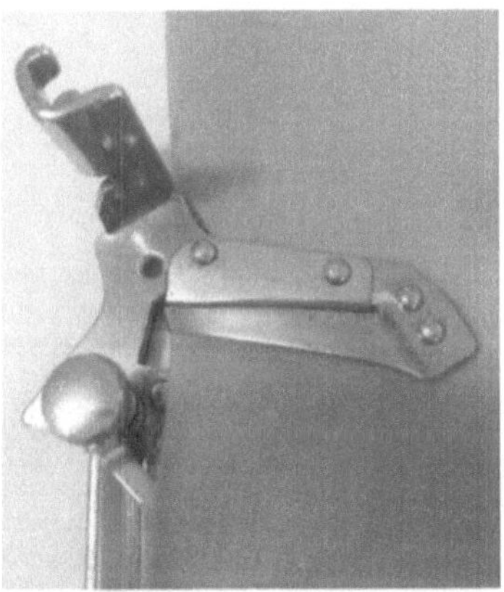

TRICKS FOR USING IT

Don't let all the numbers on the measuring scale intimidate you. Learning to understand the scale is worth the effort because the hemmer is so easy to use once you catch on.

A large screw on the left of the attachment is key. Loosen this to move, tighten, and set the metal pointer so it aims at the appropriate number on the scale. Each number corresponds to a finished hem depth. Pointer settings for hem depth (in inches) are:

1/8" ¼" 3/8" ½" 5/8" ¾" 7/8" 1"

(Source: A manual of family sewing machines. Guildford, Surrey: The Singer Company (U.K.) Ltd., 1963, p. 44)

Chapter Three

THE BINDER

The binder can be used to attach pre-folded or unfolded strips of fabric to any raw edge. The vintage version of this attachment works so much better than its modern counterpart.

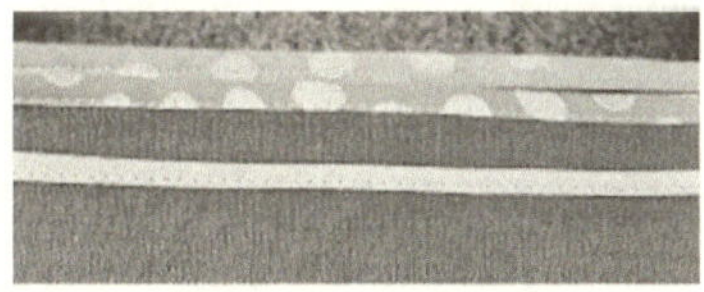

CONCEPT

Different generations of vintage binders can be sourced. The oldest, and simplest (those used on the Singer Featherweight for example) have a scroll that feeds bias strips of fabric around a raw edge of fabric as it turns under the edges of before the bias reaches the needle. Later versions of the binder, called multi-slot binders (more popular in the 1960's on), also have spaces along the scroll that will accept pre-folded binding, or any finished tape or ribbon used to bind an edge. Some of the multi-slot binders, particularly those made by Singer for slant needle machines, also have posts to help the binding feed into the attachment:

Tricks for using it

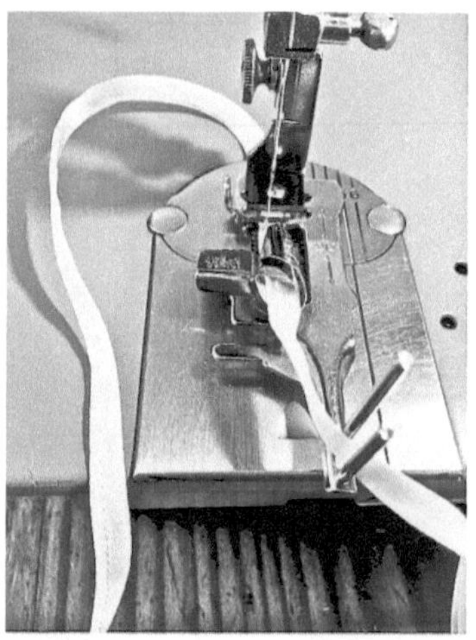

If you are getting used to a binder it is probably easier to practice first with purchased pre-folded bias binding. Purchased binding, although not always made of spectacular fabric, usually has sizing added to make it stiffer and therefore easier to feed through the unit without a lot of attention. This can be replicated in any fabric by spray starching custom-made binding and pressing under a fold along each long edge.

Once at the machine, the binder can be adjusted by either a screw or level to move it to either the right or left so the needle will fall closely to the edge to be bound.

As with most attachments holding the binding up slightly,

at a 45-degree angle, rather than flat to the bed of the machine, will make feeding the binding into the scroll easier.

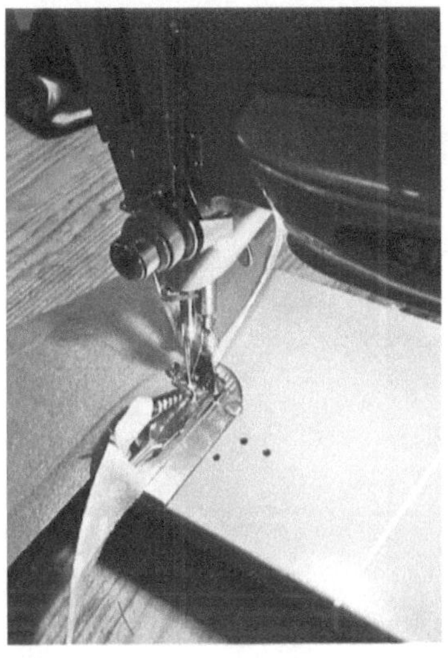

THE BUTTONHOLER

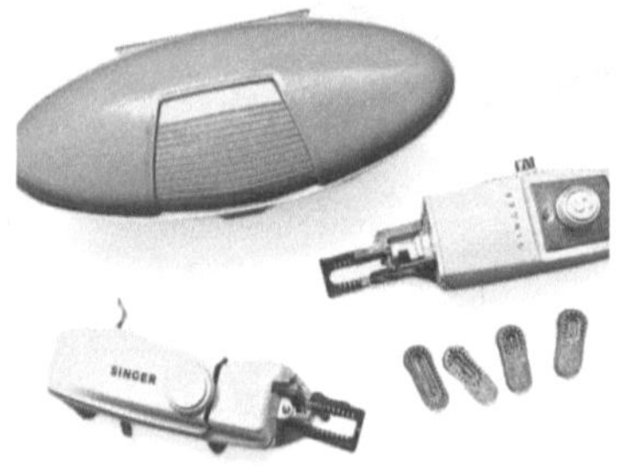

There are essentially two generations of buttonhole attachments. These are those that were built for machines up to the 1960s and load the templates on the underside of the device, and those manufactured later that loaded the templates at the top. The top-loading versions, which usually fit machines of any vintage, are more convenient as they allow the sewist to change template sizes without having to remove the entire unit from the machine and turn it over.

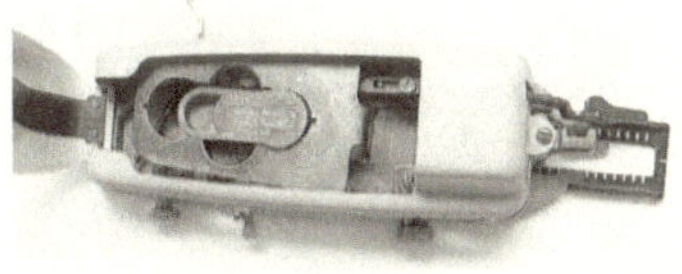

Template driven buttonhole attachments make amazing buttonholes with next to no effort.

Older templates are made of metal and come in a variety of sizes for both conventional and keyhole buttonholes. Note that they, like the later generation of templates, only produce buttonholes with rounded ends, not the bar-tack versions modern machines make. These older metal templates can also be used in top-loading newer buttonholers.

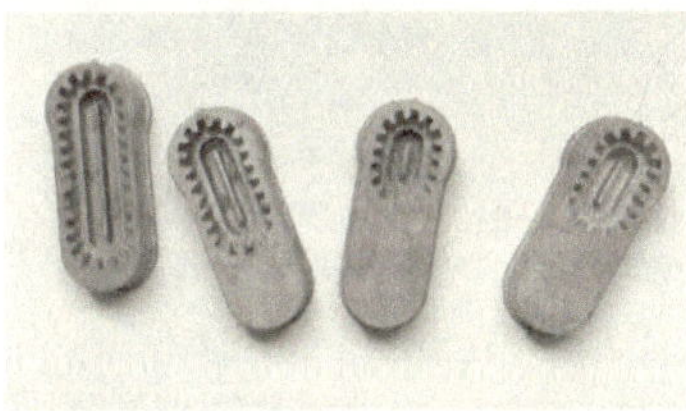

The buttonhole templates of the 1960s were made of plastic, in a wider range of sizes and styles. Those for standard garment buttonholes look like this:

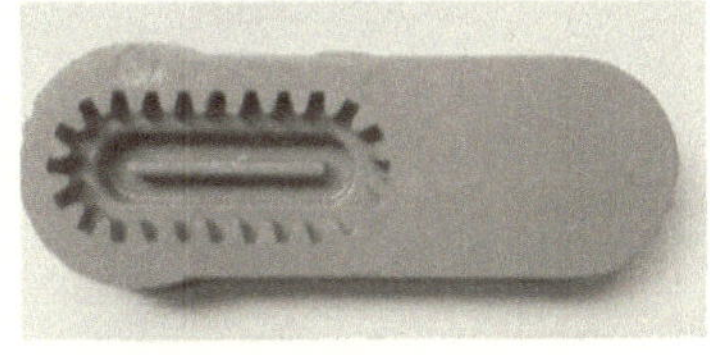

For keyhole buttonholes like this:

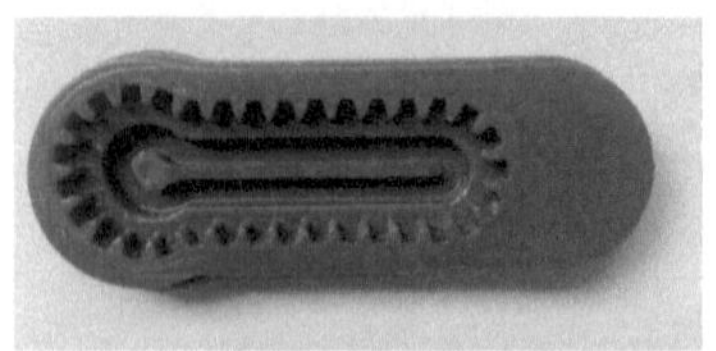

And for bound buttonholes like this with a raised bar in the center of each template to replicate the open area between stitching:

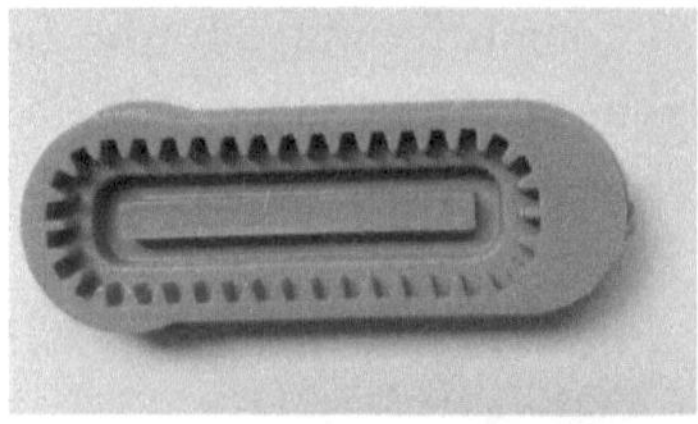

Making samples is useful when working with these templates. Here I have made a series of keyhole buttonholes with different width settings, using different templates and stitching some once, and some twice. The numbers refer to my notes for the settings for each buttonhole:

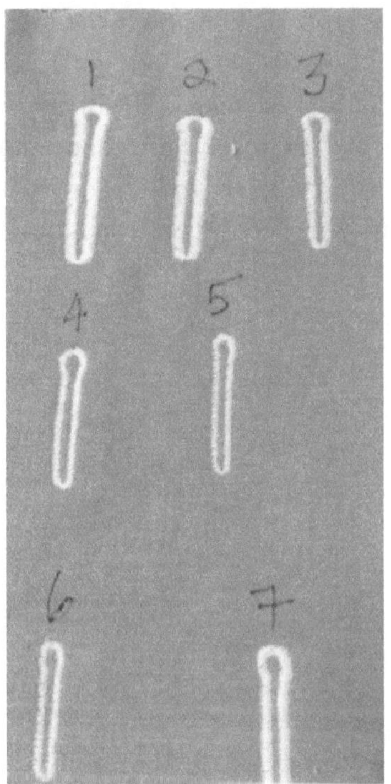

CONCEPT

Driven by the gear principle, these buttonholes are defined by unalterable shapes and sizes set by the template chosen. Stitches are never crooked or off course.

USES

Obviously, these attachments can be used anywhere button-holes are needed, but I find them particularly useful when sewing heavier fabrics, when tailoring, or when working with fine finishes. I also think round-ended buttonholes are beautiful and that the ability to sew around several times, with perfect accuracy, gives superior coverage for fabrics that can ravel.

The bound buttonhole templates are my favorites.

These available for top-loading buttonholes are not as famous as they should be. Templates, in my opinion, are the best way to make perfectly consistent button buttonholes with simplicity and precision.

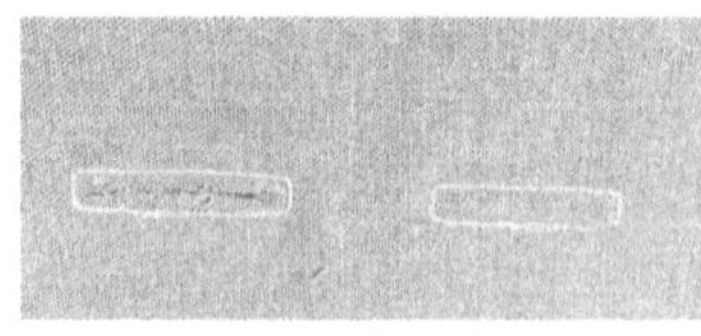

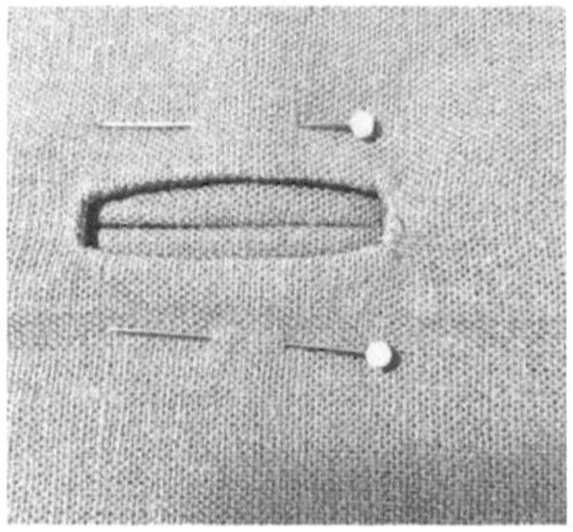

HOW THEY WORK

Older Singer and Geist black buttonhole makers designed for straight stitch machines like the Featherweight that do not do a zigzag so they operate with a straight stitch, and move the unit sideways to create the satin stitching. These are the buttonholers with metal templates.

To use these buttonholers the feed dogs are covered, and the templates are inserted in the bottom of the unit before the attachment is fixed to the machine. The knob at the top is turned until the finger-like cloth clamp is at the top of the buttonhole is just a stitch or two to the right of the marked center of the opening. Once the cloth clamp is in this position a single stitch is taken to bring the bobbin thread to the surface of the fabric, a few stitches are made, and the thread is clipped. After this, all the sewist has to do is put her foot on the foot control and watch. The buttonhole can be stitched once or around a second time, depending on how firm a buttonhole is and how much thread coverage is required.

When the stitching is completed, the top thread is pulled to the underside of the fabric, tied off, and trimmed.

The more complex setup for newer (1960s) top-loading units is described below.

Settings for all types of buttonholes

Disengaging the feed dogs

Most buttonholers require the feed dogs to be disabled as it is the unit and not the feed dog teeth that move the fabric. Most often, and always with bottom loading units, this is done by attaching a screw-on cover over the feed dogs, This plate comes with the accessory.

Newer 1960s+ "Singer Professional" beige, buttonholers, designed for slant and vertical needle bars machines often alternately allow for the feed dogs to be simply lowered. This is done by a special throat plate lever on the right side of the bed of the machine.

Setting width for each style of unit:

1. A lever at the side of bottom loading buttonholers to be used with straight stitch machines sets the width of the satin stitching. The settings are from N (narrow) through 1-6 to W (wide). The cutting area in the middle of these buttonholes is adjusted proportionally and automatically.

2. In newer model buttonholers, the top-loading style designed to be used with zigzag machines, the width of the satin stitch sides is set at the machine as a zigzag. The machine settings for these buttonholers are:

   - Needle position, set at center, if this is an option on the model.
   - Stitch width setup depends on the machine model. In the Rocketeer this is done by moving the stitch selection dials to A L and using the stitch width selections. In other models, the stitch width dials are used. Stitch width can be anything in the range of 2-4 as set on the machine.
   - Cutting space stitch width is set on the front left-hand side of the buttonhole unit itself. Sample tests and fine-tuning are useful and remember that heavier fabrics = wider stitch width = wider cutting space. I love the option to set cutting width in the middle of a buttonhole. So many contemporary "automatic" buttonholes have such a tiny cutting area that it is hard not to cut through the satin stitches when trying to slash open a finished buttonhole.
   - Set the stitch length selector- this is on the rear left side of the unit, behind the cutting space lever. The number 1 is the standard setting for a nice satin stitch but may be too dense when working with heavy fabrics. In that case, move the lever closer to the 2 setting until the unit stitches and moves easily.

TRICKS FOR USING IT

The raised bar in the center of each template represents the cutting area of the buttonhole and is useful for determining which buttonhole will fit a button. Note the test samples need to be stitched in the same number of fabric layers, including interfacing, as the garment.

Cotton embroidery thread makes the nicest buttonholes with good coverage. I always loosen the upper tension too, so the lock stitch is pulled to the underside of the fabric, creating a nice smooth satin stitch surface.

For the most elegant, custom-like buttonhole, sewists were often advised to go around the buttonhole first with a wide stitch width and then again over the top of that with a narrower stitch width. This technique was ambitiously named the "purl buttonhole" method in vintage sales literature.

THE EDGE STITCHER

CONCEPT

The edge-stitcher is an ingenious device made of a series of slots used to position trims with a very slight overlap so they can be stitched down quickly, easily, accurately, and very, very close to the edge – all without pinning or measuring.

HOW IT WORKS

The edge stitcher can be used and understood visually once you notice that the fabric insertion slots on each edge are slightly offset. This means that any two trims, or even folded fabric edges, can be inserted, one on each side, and straight stitched together with a row of stitching evenly, but breathtakingly, right at the edge of the material on the top. Experiment to discover the full potential of this function.

USES

The edges to be joined may include edge-to-edge laces or ribbons, lace edging to a folded hem, and ribbon or braid trim applied under a folded edge (military-type braids).

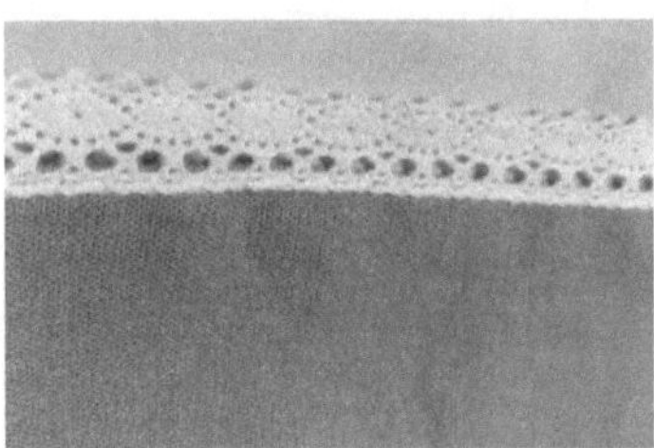

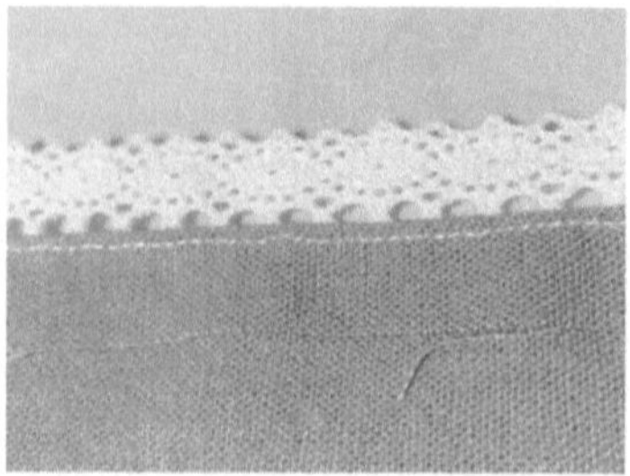

Additionally, a center slot in the foot can be used to insert narrow trims, either alone or while other materials are being joined.

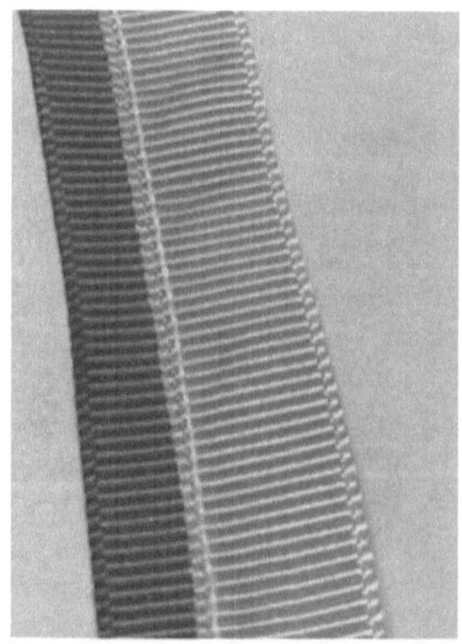

The foot can also be used to efficiently make French seams, without pinning or trimming with this three-step process:

1. Feed two layers of fabric, right sides together, through the top left-hand slot.

2. Turn and press this seam right sides together, encasing the raw edges.

3. Right sides together feed the fabric again through the edge stitcher, in either the first or second slot, and stitch.

THE MONOGRAMMER

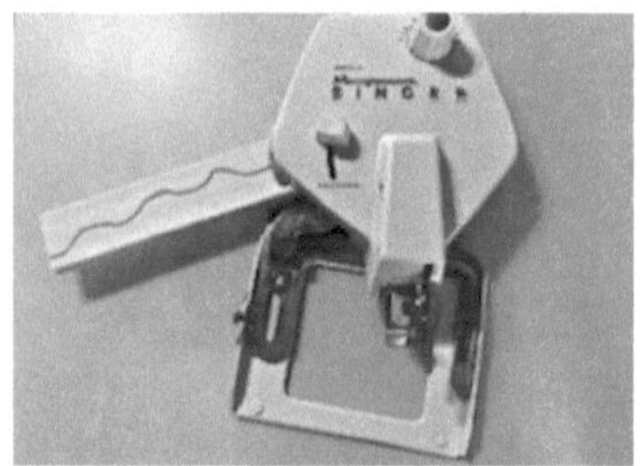

CONCEPT

The monogrammer is definitely one of the quirkier of the vintage sewing machine attachments. It was produced by Singer for their slant needle machines in the 1960s in that tantalizing period before the development of full-scale hoop embroidery machines driven by computerized chipboards. I feel these early attachments however work as well as anything that followed.

A monogrammer is an entirely mechanical way of sewing large single embroidery letters and some decorative motifs.

Like all mechanically driven devices, it is extraordinarily precise and produces predictable results.

Each letter is 1 ½" high.

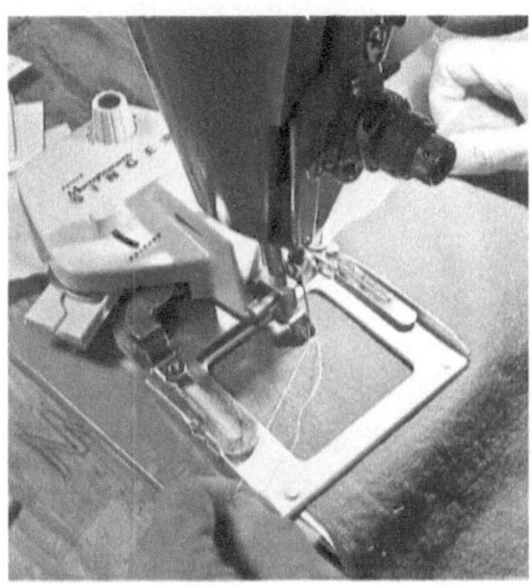

HOW IT WORK

The monogrammer operates with a series of sort of plastic rulers, called cams, that feed themselves through the box on the back of the hoop when the machine runs. These cams, one for each letter or motif (these are widely available, although fairly expensive on eBay, as individual letter purchases – if you are lucky your own initials will be included in a unit you buy), are really mechanical templates that the attachment reads like sewing braille as they travel through the machine.

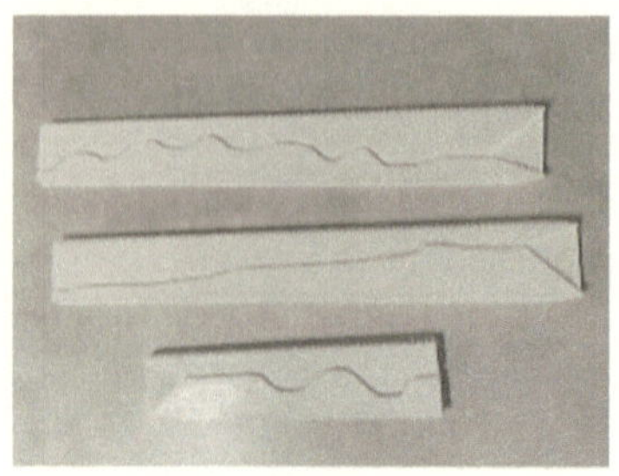

Machine set-up:

1. Drop or cover the feed-dogs.

2. Attach the unit like any other accessory making sure the fork is positioned over the needle bar screw.

3. For dense, satin stitching, move the stitch length to the "Fine setting."

4. Select the stitch width of choice – this can be none, for straight stitch monograms, or different widths for different looks – wider for heavier fabrics, narrower for finer fabrics.

5. Use the clear plastic templates, that have a needle start mark on them, to position the monogram on the fabric. Remove the templates before stitching of course.

6. Manually lower the needle into the fabric and pull up the bobbin thread before you start stitching.

7. Insert the cam into the unit and turn the cam dial clockwise until it is in the marked "start" position.

8. Stitch twice for a more defined raised monogram.

9. When the stitching is done raise the presser foot, remove the fabric, and pull both threads to the underside, knot, and cut. Turn the cam dial counterclockwise to release the cam.

Hint: if the thread breaks during the process, move the release lever (marked on the top of the unit) to the front turn the cam positioner dial counterclockwise until just before the break, and continue stitching.

TRICKS FOR USING IT

The fabric is laid under the monogrammer as if it were a giant presser foot. The feed dogs are covered or disengaged.

Due to the beautiful density of the satin stitching, it is a good idea to stabilize the fabric before stitching. This is particularly critical for finer fabrics which will have a great tendency to pull up with the stitching. In the example above, stitched on natural linen without a stabilizer, the letters are stitched well but the little flower shows some puckering around the stitches. A stabilizer, paper, a tear-away, or even an adhesive machine embroidery stabilizer would have prevented this.

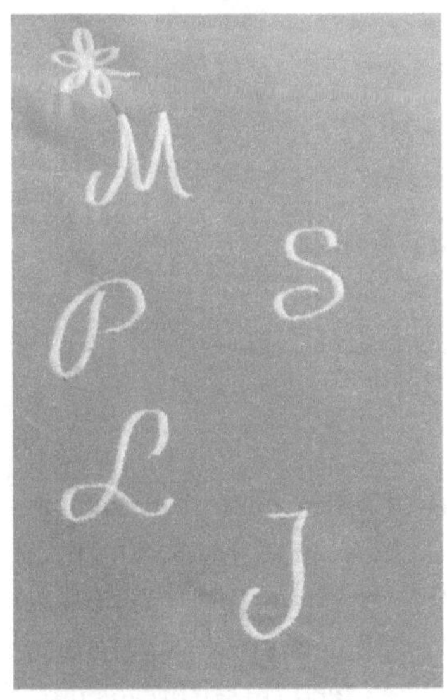

Chapter Seven

THE NARROW HEMMER

CONCEPT

The hardest part of rolled hemming is getting the fabric into the attachment. The easiest way to do this is to make a few straight stitches on the edge of the fabric, remove the fabric from under the needle, and pull out a good length of thread before it is cut. Then feed these threads into the scroll of the hemmer – like sort of a leash attached to the fabric – and pull it through. The fabric should roll in the attachment when you do this.

The next step is to hold the body of the fabric up a good few inches above the bed of the machine, up and slightly to the left, and with the fingers of your right hand roll the fabric so it feeds into the attachment.

I don't find pre-pressing the fabric under or pinning any help at all – in fact, like most of these attachments, you are better to trust and let the attachment do its job naturally.

That said, curves that will have an element of bias, or fine fabrics, are easier to feed if they have been stay-stitched close to the edge first. (See the beautiful hem made on the ruffle in the next chapter).

Chapter Eight

THE RUFFLER

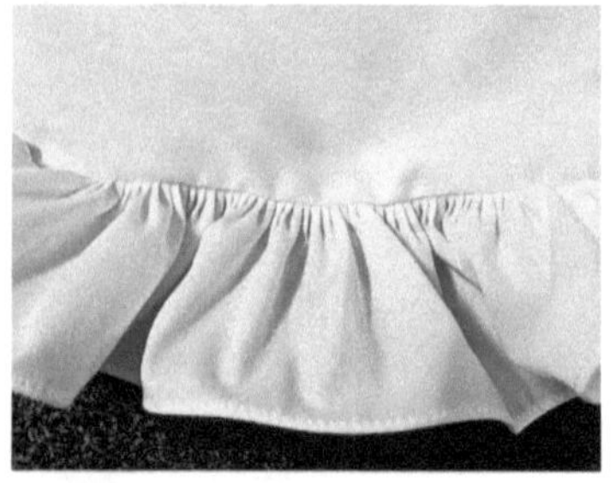

CONCEPT

The ruffler is one attachment that is still produced today in essentially the same form as the vintage models. I can't even tell the brand-new ruffler for my modern machine from the 60-year-old version I have for my Featherweight. The only difference to watch for is if the ruffler you have is either the high, low, or slant shank the machine at hand needs. I am particularly fond of a description of the ruffler in an old Singer sales brochure as able to *make ruffles of any desired fullness at a speed of ten yards in ten minutes.* (the italics are mine).

The ruffler can do these three things:

1. Gather single layers of fabric quickly and evenly, with the degree of gather adjustable.

2. Gather one layer of fabric and attach it to a flat piece of fabric at the same time.

3. Gather one layer of fabric while at the same time stitching it between two other layers of flat fabric.

With a simple adjustment, these functions can be used to pleat, rather than gather, the fabric. The pleats can be adjusted to different sizes/depths and can also be spaced – sections of straight unpleated fabric alternating with sections of pleating, with both the number and size of those spaced pleats variable.

It is also possible to do all of the above and attach piping or a narrow ribbon or trim either between or above the stitching line (slots in the top of the attachment above the ruffling/pleating mechanisms accommodate this).

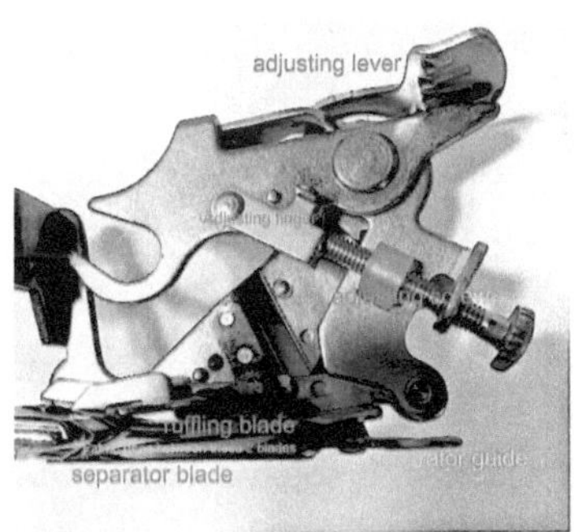

HOW IT WORKS

The ruffler operates in layers:

1. At the bottom is an S-shaped piece called the separator guide. Fabric to be ruffled goes over the first arm of the guide

and under the second arm and in between the blue separating and ruffle blades.

2. Flat fabric to which a ruffle or pleat is to be attached also goes over and then under the separator guide but does not go between the separating and ruffling blades but underneath the separating blade, next to the feed dogs. The separating blade keeps the flat fabric from ruffling. Note ruffles can also be sewn flat onto a large area of fabric by stitching down the center of each ruffle strip, as in the front of a ruffled blouse.

3. Next above the separating guide are two blue blades, the separating blade, and the ruffling blade. Fabric fed between these will be ruffled, gathered, or pleated. The upper blue ruffling blade, the one with the little teeth on it, is the active part of the attachment that actually does the work of ruffling or pleating by arranging the fabric as it reaches the needle.

The large adjusting screw at the front of the attachment determines the degree of gather in the ruffle by varying the pressure on the fabric (tighten the screw for more gathering, loosen for less).

Hint: When making large pleats this screw can be tightened until it stops up right against the adjusting finger.

To sew a row of ruffles between two layers of flat fabric:

Feed the fabric into the ruffler in these layers:

1. One layer of flat fabric over the first part of the separator guide and under the second part and then under the separator blade so it lies under the whole attachment next to the feed dogs.

2. The layer to be ruffled is placed over the first part of the separator guide and under the second part and then in between the separator blade and the ruffling blade.

3. The second layer of flat fabric is laid over both parts of the separator guide, over all other layers and under the

presser foot −the one with the central hole for feeding through tape or ribbon.

Lower the presser foot lever and off you go.

Making use of the ruffling blade

The ruffling blade is also controlled by the settings, marked by slots in the adjusting lever, the little plate with the slots you can see at the top of the attachment.

The ruffling blade is also controlled by the settings, marked by slots in the adjusting lever, the little plate with the slots you can see at the top of the attachment.

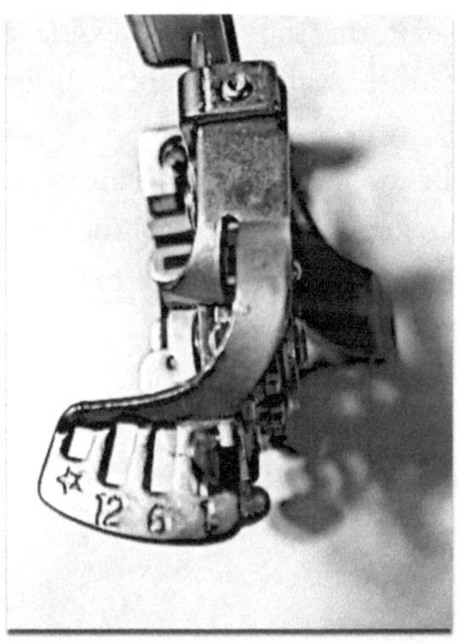

When the lever is set in the right slot, marked 1, no pleats are made, and the attachment will make only ruffles. When set at the next slot to the left, marked 6, the machine will make a 1/8" pleat every six stitches, when set at 12 it will make a pleat every 12 stitches. This spacing can be fine-tuned and adjusted of course by changing stitch length as well. Finally, on the very left the slot marked with the star will suspend all pleating action and the machine will just straight stitch. This setting was popular in making vintage trims when small sections of pleats were spaced evenly between flat sections of fabric. To space the groupings of pleats evenly sewists were often advised to count the straight stitches between pleated sections.

Tricks for using it

In addition to determining the degree of gather in a ruffle or the depth of a pleat by adjusting the adjusting screw, changing the stitch length can make a real difference in results too. A longer stitch length will produce a more gathered ruffle and larger pleats; a shorter stitch length will produce less pronounced gathering and smaller pleats.

Also, fabric cut on the more flexible cross grain will gather and pleat more easily than fabric cut on the lengthwise grain.

This lady's dickey made from a vintage pattern has used the binder for the neckline finish and the side ties, a ruffle for the tiers, and the edge stitcher to attach lace edging to the short ends of the ruffle.

Chapter Nine

THE SHIRRING FOOT

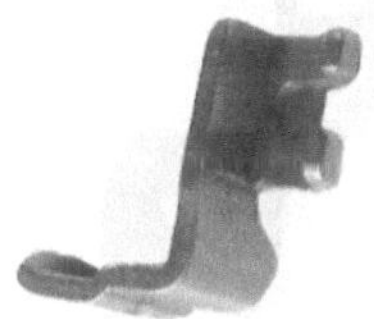

Concept

Unlike the ruffler, which really is an attachment that gathers fabric in the traditional sense, the shirring foot softly gathers light fabrics only and is most effective when used to create rows of shirred fabric. For appropriate expectations don't expect this foot to gather.

USES

Think of areas of a garment that could be smocked – upper bust areas of blouses, cuffs, and yokes. Hand-winding elastic thread in the bobbin will produce entire areas of stretchy shirred fabric – as you might find in the bodices of sundresses.

HOW IT WORKS

Like most vintage attachments the shirring foot works by exaggerating the natural mechanics of a sewing machine, in this case, the regular motion of the teeth of the feed dogs. The shirring foot is distinguished by an extra thick foot area that presses the fabric hard into the feed dogs so each stitch is picked up and slightly pleated. So simple, although only effective when working with single layers of thin fabric in proportion to the tiny teeth.

TRICKS FOR USING IT

Plan to use this foot to sew multiple rows of shirring – ¼" apart works very well – to create the appearance of machine smocking. Always use a straight stitch. Test of course but consider that a long stitch length, picking up more fabric, will gather more than a short stitch. Turning up the upper tension dial, and simultaneously tightening the bobbin tension to match by turning the small bobbin screw to the right, will also increase the degree of gather. Note for stitch quality balancing the tension, and turning them both up, is help

Chapter Ten

THE TUCKER

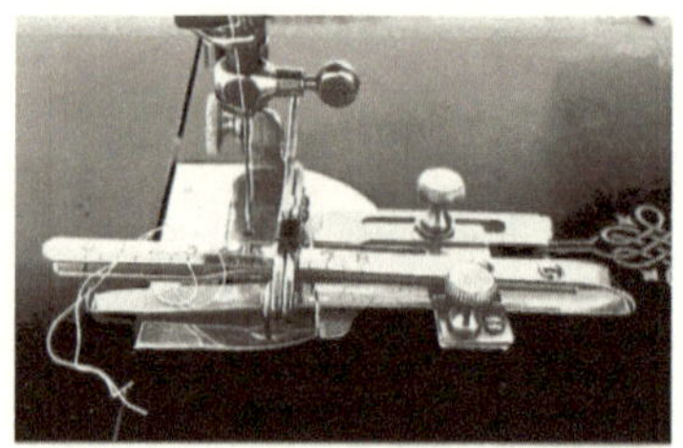

CONCEPT

Although the tucker can look like one of the more horrifyingly complex of the attachments, it is in fact one of the simplest and certainly the most ingenious.

It has two functions:

1. To line up a folded edge of fabric for even stitching from that fold – this will form a tuck.

2. To simultaneously mark the next fold line for the next tuck, ensuring that all tucks will be the same size and spaced the same distance apart.

Hint: only the first tuck needs to be measured and the tucker adjusted accordingly. All subsequent tucks can be accurately stitched by simply folding the fabric along the fold line marked while the previous tuck was being stitched.

Beautiful rows of tucks like these on my mother's christening gown, made, I am sure with a tucking attachment by my grandmother, can be made without measuring, pinning, or pre-pressing. Consider that.

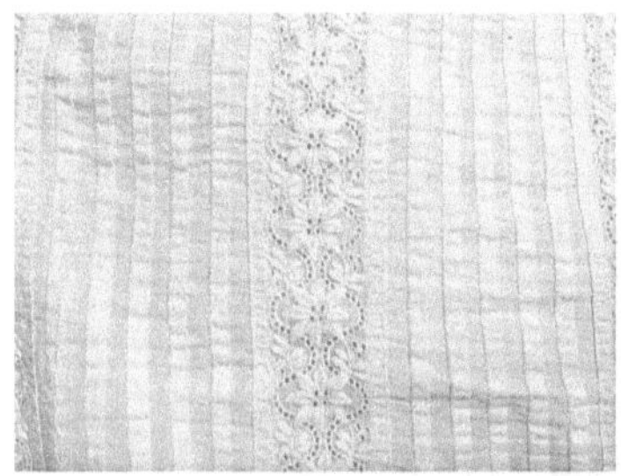

Showing far less skill but still using the tucker at its widest setting is a shirt front dickey I made from a vintage pattern:

HOW IT WORKS

The tucker is basically a set of two scales, one for establishing tuck width and one for establishing space between tucks. They each have their own adjusting screw for moving the scale into position, to be tightened before use. What is really interesting is that as you stitch the tuck, an arm set by the tuck spacing scale presses down on the fabric and creates a crease that marks the fold line for the next tuck. The beauty of marking the next tuck as you go like this is that the mark is visible but subtle and will not create any permanent mark on even the most delicate fabric. Genius.

REAR TUCK WIDTH SCALE

This is marked 1-8 representing eighths of an inch. The scale is moved until the needle position is lined up with the selected tuck width. As the stitching is done this measured distance from the folded fabric this is what those tucks would be:

Setting Finished tuck width Fabric taken up by tuck

1 1/8" ¼"

2 ¼" ½"

3 3/8" ¾"

4 ½" 1"

5 5/8" 1 ¼"

6 ¾" 1 ½"

7 7/8" 1 ¾"

8 1" 2"

(Source: my tested calculations.)

FRONT TUCK SPACING SCALE

The numbers on the tuck spacing scale are interesting – although they also number 1-8 you will notice that the space between each number is twice as big as the spaces between the numbers on the tuck width scale. This is because the spacing scale each tuck will be pressed into the space between each tuck - essentially covering part of the space between each tuck with that fabric. For example, if you want to make ½" tucks spaced ½" apart then the tuck spacing scale will have to mark the next fold line 1 ½" from the stitching line of the preceding tuck. From the stitching line for preceding tuck + 1" tuck spacing (1/2" of that covered by the preceding tuck, ½" of that showing as spacing between tucks + ½" up one side of the next tuck to the fold line for that next ½" tuck) = 1 ½"

If this explanation seems complicated, use this formula instead:

Tuck size (1/8") Spacing between tucks (None) Tuck width (1") Tuck space (1")

Tuck size (1/8") Spacing between tucks (1/8") Tuck width (1") Tuck space (1")

Tuck size (1/8") Spacing between tucks (None) Tuck width (1") Tuck space (1 ½")

Tuck size (1/4") Spacing between tucks (1 1/4") Tuck width (2") Tuck space (3")

Tuck size (1/2") Spacing between tucks (None) Tuck width (4") Tuck space (4")

Tuck size (1/2") Spacing between tucks (1/2") Tuck width (4") Tuck space (6")

Tuck size (1/8") Spacing between tucks (None) Tuck width (8") Tuck space (8")

(Source: *A manual of family sewing machines.* Guildford, Surrey: The Singer Company (U.K.) Ltd., 1963, p. 48)

TRICKS FOR USING IT

Set the tucker for both the width of the tuck and the space between each tuck. Finger press the first tuck along its length, being careful to keep that fold along the grain of the fabric – this will keep the tuck from twisting. Feed the tuck into the tucker being careful to keep the fold right up into the right side of the attachment. Lower the presser foot and stitch, noting that as you do so the next tuck is being marked. When you are stitching the last tuck raise the tuck space lever so the fabric will not be marked further.

Hint: As with many attachments I find it more sensible to use the tucker to make a tucked piece of fabric first and then use it to cut out the garment piece.

Chapter Eleven

THE ZIPPER FOOT

The best for almost last.

The modern zipper foot is to my mind a case of replacing something that works with something that doesn't. Key to the installation of a beautiful zipper, or to make piping, is the ability to place the machine stitches close to the teeth. Here are two older feet I use frequently:

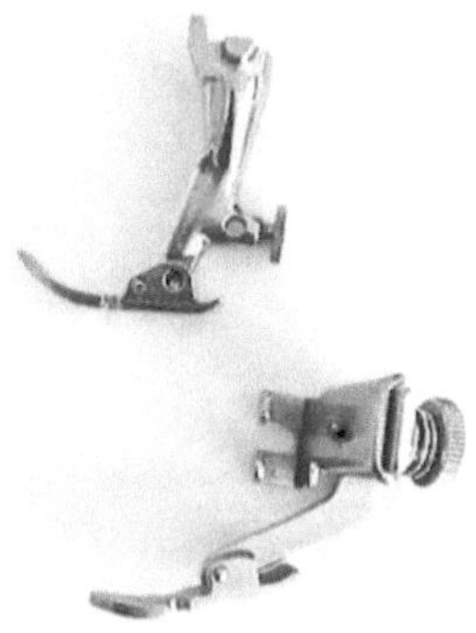

Vintage zipper feet do this very well by having the foot

itself able to slide to one side, as in the case of this low shank older Singer foot:

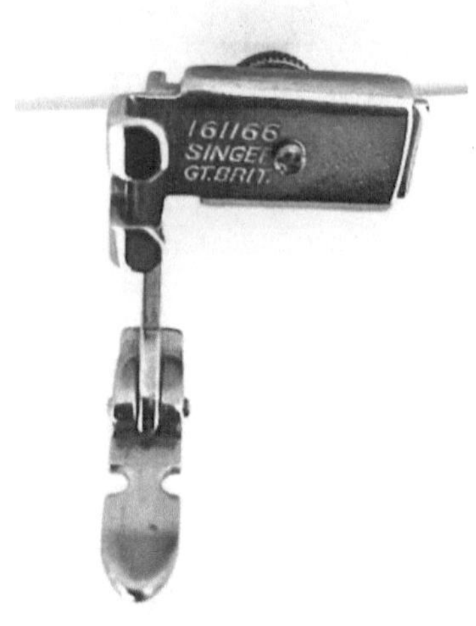

Hint: On some machines instead of the slider, the machine's ability to adjust needle position for either side of the foot, as in this Bernina Old Style foot can be used instead:

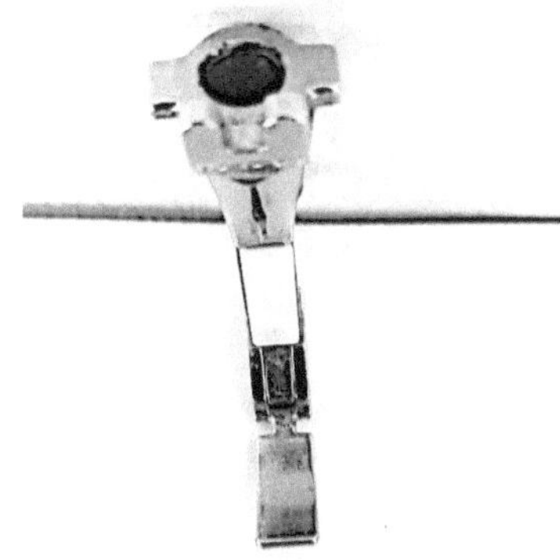

The concept of using needle position shifts has been carried on in many modern feet. However, the feet that are snapped onto the machine all tend to be far wider than the vintage editions. In practice this wider foot often pushes the zipper to one side, and away from the stitches. I have seen this happen again and again in my sewing classes and observed the frustration this foot design has produced in my students. The difference to me between a vintage zipper foot and a modern one is like the difference between a shovel and a snowplow. You can see what I mean below in these two examples of contemporary zipper feet:

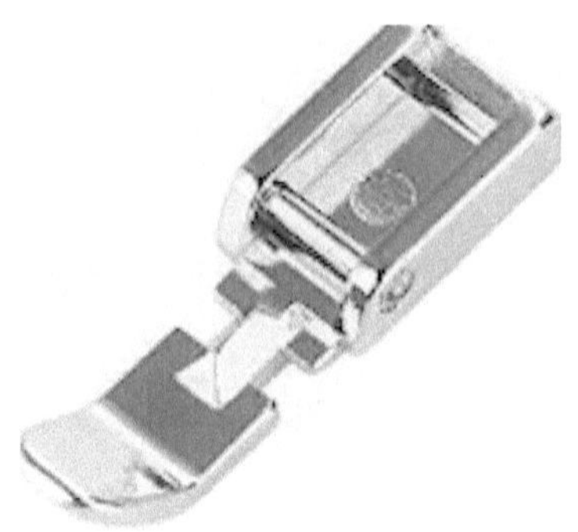

Chapter Twelve

EMBROIDERY CAMS

Although these are not strictly sewing machine attachments, I feel that something should be said about the cam system Singer introduced in the 1960s to allow pre-computerized machines to sew a variety of embroidery or "utility" stitches.

As with other template or gear-driven mechanisms like the buttonholer and the monogrammer, the rigor of the embroidery cams produces relentlessly uniform stitches. Here are some of the cams in my collection:

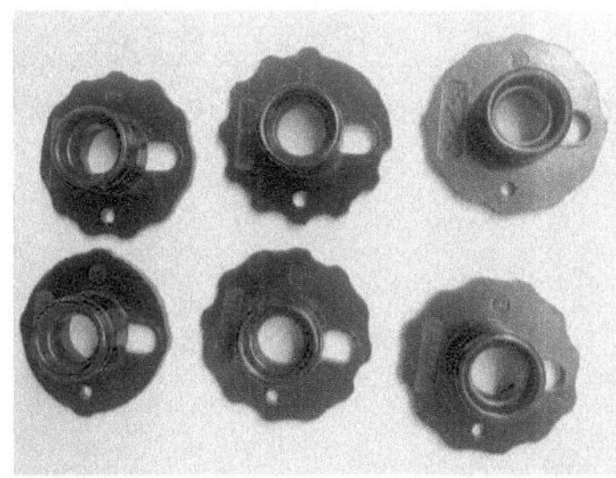

An inserted into the top of my Rocketeer:

And the underside of the machine lid which gives operating instructions:

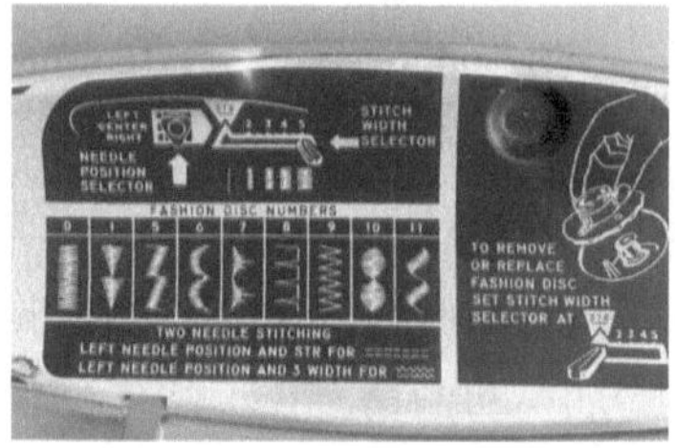

Stitch samples of a large number of the designs possible with cams can be found here on Elena's wonderful vintage sewing blog.

....

BEST WISHES

....

This little book comes from the notes I have made in my own sewing room. It a personal project written with the hope that the wisdom and resources of sewists past can make many complex sewing tasks just a little bit easier for those of us who carry on the tradition of original garment making today.

Thank you so much for sharing your interest in our craft with me.

Happy sewing,

Barbara

Barbara Emodi sews and writes cozy mysteries set in Nova Scotia, Canada. Gasper's Cove doesn't *really* exist but it will seem awful familiar to anyone who lives where she does. The community is based all she believes matters in life - extended family, companion animals, good food, and more sewing, crafting, quilting, and knitting projects than any reasonable person would take on.

Her sewing books are an expression a lifetime spent learning from other garment-makers and passing on this heritage of knowledge to those learning to sew.

Her fiction reflect what she likes to read - whimsical, witty, warm books, that reflect her belief that there is nothing ordinary about ordinary people. She also likes clever surprises, important in mysteries, and promises one at the end of each book. To visit Gasper's Cove yourself you can read Barbara's novels in her **Gasper's Cove Mysteries** series or her **Gasper's Cove Quick Cozies** novella series.

For writing updates and ***for subscribers only*** advance peeks at new books, free stories, and, most important, her husband's cooking secrets, sign up here for her newsletters at babsemodi.com

And remember the best way to support an author is to leave a review. Stars or/and words help other readers find their way to Gasper's Cove.

To get to know Barbara better you can also read her Substack column ***How to be an Older Woman for Beginners.***

My readers are with me when I write.
    Contact me directly by email any time.
    barbara@babsemodi.com

ALSO BY BARBARA EMODI

Novels:

Gasper's Cove Mysteries

Crafting for Murder

Crafting for Deception

Crafting for Slander

Crafting a Getaway

Crafting an Alibi Coming April 2025

Crafting a Cold Case Coming Fall 2025

Novellas:

Gasper's Cove Quick Cozies check revised ASIN numbers

Panic in the Pansies

Inspection Deception

Potions and Notions

Last Stitch Effort

Non-fiction: Sewing Books

SEW: the garment-making book of knowledge

Stress-free Sewing Solutions

Vintage Sewing Machine Attachments for the Modern Sewist